Other books by Patricia Taylor Wells

The Eyes of the Doe

Mademoiselle Renoir à Paris

Lodestar

The Sand Rose

Kaleidoscope

Patricia Taylor Wells

GusGus Press • Bedazzled Ink Publishing
Fairfield, California

© 2022 Patricia Taylor Wells

All rights reserved. No part of this publication may be reproduced
or transmitted in any means,
electronic or mechanical, without permission in
writing from the publisher.

978-1-949290-95-0 paperback

Cover Design
by

GusGus Press
a division of
Bedazzled Ink Publishing Company
Fairfield, California
http://www.bedazzledink.com

For those who
have forgotten how to love

Kaleidoscope is a collection of poems representing life's everchanging views. Patricia Taylor Wells shares the changing patterns of a world darkened by a pandemic, the loss of her mother, and other events that brought uncertainty to her life. But she also reveals the healing power of nature and the hidden beauty behind every cloud of doubt. The poet takes particular delight with her metaphoric descriptions of the natural, material, and spiritual worlds reflected throughout this collection.

Sun, Moon, and Stars

Morning Star   11
Beautiful World   12
Stars   13
Full Moon   14
The Far Side of the Moon   15
Harvest Moon   17
The Great Conjunction   18

Morning Star

Just before sunrise,
Low in the Eastern sky,
The Morning Star shines brightly—
Rivaled only by the moon.
It hangs like a lantern in the air,
Its fiery glow unflinching—
A dazzling ray of hope,
As darkness fades to light.
Washed away by daytime,
It wanders far away
Pausing as the sun sets
To woo the Western sky.

Beautiful World

When the stars against a dark sky
Shine their mellow light on dew,
And the moon, just past its Harvest,
Has begun its life anew;
When the Autumn song of robins
Is heard at early dawn,
And the leaves are changing colors
Beneath a haloed sun;
When the summer blooms have wilted
And a cool air whips our way,
My heart is filled with rapture—
Oh, World! You're much too beautiful today.

Stars

On a skyway in the heavens
Once day has lost its Light,
The moon begins to take its place
To host the dark of night.
As the stars come out and mingle
A comet passes by,
Followed by a starry band
That shoots across the sky.
Down the lane, an art museum
Features constellations
Which have lived in the Milky Way
Ever since Creation.
Orion, with his hunting bow,
His star-lit belt and sword;
Pegasus with his wings held high
Galloping like a lord;
When Aquarius spills his jar
He causes quite a splash,
And Phoenix in the Southern sky
Arises from the ash.
The sky's celestial compass
 Polaris points the way
To anywhere you want to go
From dark till break of day.
And if you wish upon a star
You must not hesitate,
For once, the Sun King wakes the morn
The stars all hibernate.

Full Moon

The moon, illuminated by the sun,
Climbs slowly in the sky.
Closer now to Earth, like a yellow sphere
Pasted against a black wall sprinkled with stars,
Surrounded by a halo that weeps a silver light.
High up in the heavens, guarding against dark,
It heralds the coming of Spring.
The ground below begins to thaw
And earthworms crawl out of hiding.
A thousand times and more
We see this ritual played,
But each and every time
It always seems brand new.

The Far Side of the Moon

The moon in its orbit of the world
Mirrors Earth's dance with the sun,
Gyrating from west to east
Like a calendar in the sky,
Sun and Earthshine light its face,
And Earth then casts a shadow
That makes it wax and wane.
The moon and sun play tug-of-war
With the tidal waves onshore
That lock the moon's rotation
To the time it orbits Earth.
When Earth's between the sun and moon,
A full moon will appear,
And magically rise above a hill
Seeming larger than it is,
With dark spots all across its face
That map its lunar crust.
But what about the far side,
The part we cannot see?
Its face is full of craters
From star-wars long ago,
And sound waves are obstructed
By the mass inside its womb.
The only time its face is dark
Is when the moon we see is full.
The moon, like many things,
Is not all black or white;

And if we'd truly fancy
The far side of the moon,
We'd look right past its Dark side
And see its hidden Light.

Harvest Moon

Close to the horizon
The moon lights up the sky
And bids hello to Fall,
As Summer says goodbye.
Rising before sunset
For three nights in a row,
How could we ever tire
Of being in its glow?
The moonbeams kiss the fields
While farmers harvest crops
To feed them through Winter—
They work away, nonstop.
The moon shines so brightly
The stars cannot be seen.
Though not too far away,
Against a darkened screen
In its dazzling debut
We can see planet Mars—
Thus, when the moon is full,
What need have we for stars?

The Great Conjunction

The North pole points away from the sun,
Sinking it lower in the sky.
The day is short, and the night is long,
And the Earth, as quiet as a sigh.
Jupiter, like a majestic god,
Adorned with rings and many moons
Waltzes toward the sun with Saturn
In a grand, galactic ballroom.
As the two move slowly and closer,
Saturn's brilliant rings of ice
Burst into a shimmering rainbow
As bending sun rays are enticed.
For centuries, the orbs have danced apart,
But tonight, they will be married.
And everyone on the Earth will watch
Once the sun is set and buried.
Their cosmic kiss will ignite the sky
And the world will feel the power
Of a new age dawning in the air,
 And know this moment is ours.

Seasons

Spring   21
Summer Day   22
Endless Summer   23
Summer Evening   24
September Summer   25
Open Window   26
The Last Leaf   27
Winter Garden   28
Winter Fog   29
The Snow Storm   30
Winter Freeze   31
The Ragged Remains of Winter   32
Dour Aftermath   33

Spring

The Sun rests briefly
Between two hemispheres
Wrapped in equal day and night,
As Earth nods in its direction—
Coaxing the cosmic star to journey
Across the northern sky.
Soon the Earth will begin to thaw
And rivers and streams will flood,
Overwhelmed by melting snow.
Gradually the ground relaxes,
As the crocus and daffodil
Shyly peek at morning sun.
The trees sprout gowns of green
To keep us cool and clean the air.
Bunnies bounce across the lawn
And birds sing sweet refrains,
As bees and butterflies
Compete for colors
That draw them to the bloom.
As the days grow longer
And the sky is painted blue—
The weariness of Winter
Fades, even in our hearts,
And our eyes open wide
To all that's new
As we embrace the Spring.

Summer Day

An early morning rain cools the air,
And licks the grass with its tongue
Till each blade stands at attention,
Tall and unafraid.
Soon the sun burns through the clouds
Like a wildfire in the sky,
And little puddles are dried away
By its heat and blinding glare.
The day grows ever longer,
And all is slow and tired,
Unwinding like a lazy stream
That stays a steady course.
At last, the sun begins to sink,
Casting shadows on the ground.
Cicadas sing their chorus,
And birds on tender branch
Call to one another,
Then chase the fading light.
Another day has ended,
Its troubles swept away—
Yet still, I wait and wonder
What will tomorrow bring?

Endless Summer

Nothing lasts as long as summer,
When even the dog lies still
And does not chase,
And birds perch quietly
In the shade of branch,
Or the bees that are idled
By a summer dearth
Cannot find a bloom
To overcome their plight.
The Earth tilts toward the sun,
Now high as it can be,
And the fields begin to whither
From heat and lack of rain
As the unforgiving air
Paints the sky with haze.
I feel the guilt of privilege
As I sit inside and chill
While others toil beneath a sun
That drenches them with sweat.
And yet, with its discomfort,
Summer brings delight—
Swimming in the cool of lake,
Or lying on a beach,
Or napping in a hammock,
Waiting for summer's end.

Summer Evening

When daylight fades, as it must,
And the sky turns tawny peach,
The birds flirt their wings and tails
And the squirrels play hide-and-seek.
The butterflies have all gone home
To hold their wings upright,
Katydids disguised as leaves
Foretell next Autumn's frost.
The heat is strangled by a breeze,
And the shade of trees grows wide.
But soon, the world will fall asleep
And the moon will dance with the stars.

September Summer

September always lingers,
It will not quietly fade,
It seems as if it's endless
And tries to masquerade
The laziness of August,
When all we did was play,
And nothing seemed to matter,
On any given day.
For now, enjoy its pleasure
Before the Autumn tease,
Although it's hot and humid,
And doesn't bring much ease.
Still, we wait impatiently—
When will the season turn?
Not till the summer curtseys
To signal its adjourn.

Open Window

I sit by an open window
Enjoying Autumn's breeze,
And as I look all around me
The whole World seems appeased.
The squirrels chase one another
For acorns on the ground,
While wind chimes fluttering the air
Serve charismatic sound.
The leaves are starting to tarnish
But still cling tight to trees,
Though the sun has given notice
To butterflies and bees
To find a winter hiding place
Before the flowers fade.
And the birds are busy packing,
Their plans, already made
To fly away to warmer climes
Where they can live with ease.
I love this time of year because
It always seeks to please.
As I look outside my window
The World begins to change,
But its creatures are not worried—
For all is prearranged.

The Last Leaf

The sun rises beneath pinkened clouds,
Shining like a spotlight through
Branches where only a few leaves
Cling tenaciously against the wind,
Knowing that they, too, will eventually
Join the clutter on the ground—
A patchwork of crumpled life,
As mottled as a speckled hen.
A wisp of wind downs the last leaf,
It obediently yields to Nature's plot.
And the naked branches now reveal
The skeletal remains of an erstwhile nest
That was once a happy home.

Winter Garden

I love the beauty of winter—
Bare branches are like the arms
of a graceful ballerina,
Swaying slightly in the air.
And the garden's muted palette
Is as hushed as a deer in snow.
The sun, now lower in the sky,
Soaks the atmosphere,
Newly painted brilliant blue;
And cardinals red as berries
Punctuate the scenery
As they flit from tree to tree.
Ah, the solace of winter
On a lovely afternoon
Is the only thing that's needed
To warm the coldest heart.

Winter Fog

The cold, damp air hugs the ground
And rises above the lake like a smoldering fire.
The sky is draped in a grey vapor,
That shrouds a reluctant sun;
And treetops stretch above
The low-lying clouds that cloak
Their skirts of green.
The world, now wrapped in gloom,
Must wait a tender while
Until its veil is lifted
By a more insistent sun.

The Snow Storm

The clouds, high and whispy, streak across the sky,
Dropping a veil over the sun, moon, and stars.
Birds puff their feathers and congregate in trees
And squirrels harvest acorns found on the ground.
The smoke curls slowly from the tops of chimneys
As everyone awaits the coming storm.
The clouds thicken and spread out like a blanket
As cold air rises, expands, and then freezes.
The shrubs and small trees are bent and paralyzed
By the arctic blast as sleet pelts the windows
And snow glazes pavement like powdered sugar.
Rooftops drizzled with icing between shingles
Shiver beneath the cold, whitewashed troposphere.
All is still and hushed as stars throughout the day,
But the evening brings a whisper of snow—
A winter lullaby in the dark of night
As snowflakes mingling gracefully in the air,
Paint Earth's canvas as a Winter Wonderland.
When the morning breaks, clouds begin to shred,
Unveiling the sun against a sky of blue.
When its rays of light shine down like golden rain,
The ground sparkles like a frozen diadem.
Snowcapped bushes masquerade as cotton fields
And birds eat all the berries on the hollies.
While the winter storm pauses, it's far from done—
Once more, we await its beauty and revenge.

Winter Freeze

The sun exhales an arctic breath
That sweeps across the Earth,
Cooling like a cosmic fan
That makes the limbs of trees
Shiver as their blood runs cold
And freezes in their veins.
Bare branches drenched in icy rain
Shine like frosted filigree,
While evergreens fold their boughs
To shed the weight of ice and snow.
The ground, now covered in a wrap
 As white as any dazzling star,
Does twinkle like a thousand eyes
Staring at the moon.

The Ragged Remains of Winter

The untarnished blanket of snow
Now glistens in the sun.
The air, still refrigerated,
Puts up a gallant fight.
Overcome by radiant heat,
Earth's icing slowly shrinks.
The temperature then rises
Above the freezing point.
The snow begins to tear apart
As if pulled from each side,
Till the ground is as mottled as
The spots of Holstein cows.
Birds gather under the hollies,
Now bare of all their fruit,
To find the berries laid to rest
Under the piles of snow.
When the Blue Jays and the Grackles
Decide to interfere
Inside the Robins' real estate,
The birds form their armies
And fan their tails like waving flags
As battle lines are drawn.
The frosted leaves of trees and shrubs
Will soon be green again.
Now, all there is are the ragged
Remains of winter's woe
 as we await the coming spring.

Dour Aftermath

Along the highway, the trees stand tall,
Their branches like skeletons
With bones broken and scattered about
What now looks like a graveyard.
The leaves, brown and crumpled by the freeze,
Cling to life, and then they fall,
And pine needles are as orange as
The manes of Safari lions.
The trees no longer shade the sun's light
Nor serve as rain umbrellas.
And through the windows of the forest
Homes, once hidden, can be viewed.
Low in the sky, mostly drained of blue,
Thin, white clouds skim by slowly.
The grass is now the color of wheat,
Where cows lie still in pastures,
And birds have lost their food and shelter,
Like all the other creatures;
Nor will the bees have blooms to gather
The nectar for their honey.
Oh, how dour—the coming spring will look
More like the dead of winter.

Creatures of the Air, Land, & Sea

Dance of the HoneyBee   37
Dragonfly   38
Ladybug Fly Away   39
Butterflies   40
The Bird   41
Barn Swallows   42
The Mockingbird   43
Blue Heron   44
Seahorses   45
Sea Shells   46
Kittens   47

Dance of the HoneyBee

I fly beneath a golden sun foraging flower clusters,
Mostly blue and violet; anything but red,
Which looks like black to me and leaves me quite uneasy.
My ultra-violet vision reveals a petal landing;
I hover close before I light and drink my fill of nectar.
I do not sting the hand that swats, for that would bring me death;
But beat my wings against the air to make a steady drone
That warns a nearby foe how fierce I'll guard my store.
I must not tarry long, for the idle Queen awaits—
As do all my sisters, who serve our wing*ed* mistress.
I quickly go back to the hive, and once inside its chamber,
I launch my dance upon its comb, mapping distance, and direction
Through *round dance* or the *waggle*,
That tells how far or near my treasured stash was found.
The others gather 'round me and imitate my moves,
Breathing in the fragrance, I carried home with me.
But soon, they take their turn and fly to where I've been,
To gather all the sweetness that's fit to feed their Queen.

Dragonfly

As nymphs, they live in water,
Sometimes a year or two
Before emerging from the deep,
Dressed in bright metallic hues.
In early mornings, they sit and sun,
In prep for taking flight,
And then they rise like acrobats
Performing in the air
Moving in all directions—up and down,
To and fro, and even side to side.
They bend and twist their wings,
And can hover for a while
like an iridescent canvas in the sky.
Their eyes are magnified
By a thousand eyes inside
So they can see in all degrees
When catching prey mid-air.
While their life is but a fraction
Of the time they spent below,
They live fully in the moment
And free of all regret.
Like tiny ballet dancers
Full of elegance and grace
They flap their gossamer wings
For their final journey home.

Ladybug Fly Away

Ladybug wears a polka dot dress
Whene'er she comes to call,
Sometimes she stays all winter
Snuggled in a wall.
But in the warmer seasons,
You'll find her on a leaf
Eating all the aphids
That brings the farmer grief.
And if you make her nervous,
She'll put up quite a stink
To make you go away
Till all her worries sink.
If food is scarce, she'll eat her own,
For her, it's not a crime
To dine upon her neighbors,
So she can reach her prime.
Before the farmer burns his fields,
He sings a little chant
For ladybug to fly away—
Not waiting till she can't;
For else her house will surely burn,
And all her children, too.
And if she never came again,
What would the farmer do?

Butterflies

The caterpillar feeds
On an emerald leaf,
While magically transformed
With each colorful molt.
As butterflies unfold
Like bright painted petals,
They then flutter in sunshine
From flower to flower—
Dancing like delicate
Little fairies with wings.
And with their long, straw-like tongues
They dine on sweet nectar
Which they taste with their feet.
Their heads have antennae
For help with their balance,
Or sensing patterns of wind,
And the fragrance of blooms.
Their feet gather pollen
When perching on flowers,
 Used to help Mother Nature
To replenish the Earth.
And when light passes through
Their wings it's reflected
As if beautiful stain glass
Decorated the air.
They never sleep but rest
By hanging upside down,
Then pasting wings together
Like folded palms in prayer.

The Bird

It blended with the mottled lawn,
Sitting still as a leaf on the ground.
Even when the dog approached,
It did not make a sound.
It stayed all alone in the open,
Its feathers puffed and cold
From the wind and rain that fell
On wings kept in a fold.
Its head would turn to the side,
As it looked through half-closed eyes,
The only sign of life,
When a bird no longer flies.
I sorrowed at its funeral,
But dared not touch its wing,
For what can we possibly do
When a bird no longer sings?
Yet a dead bird is a symbol
Of something new to come,
That takes away the darkness
And replaces it with dawn.

Barn Swallows

Each season they return,
having traveled miles on end
Over land and oceans, too.
They quickly build their nests,
Bringing joy and good fortune
To everyone it's due.
They safeguard the farms
As they hunt and feed in air,
While painting vivid hues:
White spots on tail fans
Are attractively patterned
On feathers of steely blue.
Their foreheads and throats
Like rusted clay on the ground—
What a sight they are to view.
Flying low if it rains,
And high on a sunny day,
Their predictions, always true.
And when someone has passed,
They capture their soul, then
Carry it to Heaven, too.

The Mockingbird

The mockingbird in the oleander,
Innocent of its poisonous veins,
Tap dances on its branches
As he belts out a glorious song.
Elegant in his grey coat and tail,
Set off by dark wing feathers,
Branded with white bars and patches,
Sure to please his audience.
His song is a medley of calls
He steals from the other birds,
Repeating each song that he mimics
At least three times, night or day.
Behind him is the sky;
In front, a windowsill
Where he sees his image reflected
And flings himself high in the air
To chase away his foes,
Then flutters back down to the ground
To squabble with squirrels and Blue Jays,
By fanning his tail and squawking
Until they have gone away.
And then he comes back to the window
To flirt with himself again.

Blue Heron

His widespread wings beat slow
And his neck is tucked against his shoulders.
His legs, stretched straight, trail behind him
As he strides across the sky.
He sees the lake and begins to hover,
Like a plane waiting to land,
Watching for prey and predators
Before dropping his spindly legs
Into the shallow of the lake.
He spears a fish with his bill
Then wades close to the bank,
His agile neck tightly curled.
Once he stakes his domain,
He stands alone and silent—
Extending his neck forward
And tilting his head side to side
Like a periscope when a predator
Attempts to overtake his claim.
When all is clear, he continues his wait.
A magnificent sight—his grey-blue feathers
Blending with the sky as he stands there,
Tall and statuesque, owning all he sees.

Seahorses

Seahorses glide in the ocean
As if riding a carousel.
Each morning they come together
To dance and link tails with their mate,
Then they go their separate ways—
Swimming upright with heads held high,
With dorsal fins to propel them
As they waltz and whirl in the deep,
Dressed in a bony plate armor
As delicate as filigree,
They also wear a coronet,
As though royal members at sea.
They take their curled prehensile tail
And anchor themselves to a reef
Their eyes look inverse directions
As they change their color of skin.
They then suck up food with their snouts
Like powerful vacuum cleaners.
There are many myths and legends
About seahorses around the world—
They drew Poseidon's chariot,
And they carry souls of sailors
To the underworld when they die.

Sea Shells

Wearing skeletons on their outsides
Like a suit of armor,
Clams, oysters, snails, and other mollusks
Travel the ocean floor,
Safely tucked inside their mobile home
And kept from carnivores.
But when mollusks die and decompose
The shells that they once wore
Are like coffins buried in the sand
To rest forevermore.
But oh, how lovely a shell can be,
So often, we ignore
The stylish shapes, designs, and colors
Of Nature's jewelry store.
There are clamshells hinged together
That open like a door,
Other shells are spiral or tubelike—
So many to explore.
There are cones with swirling whorls and shells
With ridges, spikes galore.
Oh, what a garden the beach can be
When seashells wash ashore.

Kittens

How can I love only one
When there are so many?
Lost, abandoned, and abused—
Some rescued barely alive.
Each has a story to tell,
But none of that seems to matter.
They come in all colors and sizes,
But in one way, they're all alike:
Love them, and they will love you back—
And the only thing they will ever ask
Is to find a forever home.

Nature's Awe

Hidden Beauty   51
Nothing's Too Small   52
Silent Rain   53
The Ocean   54
Approaching Storm   55
Hurakan   56
Force of Nature   57
The Tree   58
The Burning Tree   59
Fire   60

Hidden Beauty

Sometimes, beauty comes
From moments wrought with woe;
When clouds, dark and threatening,
Bring winds that sweep a path
Of destruction and pouring rains
That quickly drown the Earth.
But then, a rainbow's aura
blossoms like a garden in the sky
Where only splendor grows.
Or when a mountain stands before us,
And our path is wholly blocked,
Only when we reach its summit—
Does a grand, majestic view
Surface on the other side.
And even on the darkest night
When hearts are anxious and afraid,
The moon and stars still shine
Behind the clouds of doubt
That keeps us from their Light.

Nothing's Too Small

Nothing's too small to matter;
Too unimportant to exist.
A crescent moon is just as whole
As one that waxes full,
And the feeble sun that rises
Overcomes the dark of night
Like wind that's born a whisper
Yet, can blow away the world,
Or drops of rain that fall to ground
To fill the deepest sea.
The sand dunes of the desert,
Made of tiny grains of sand,
Are equally majestic
As the mountain that is formed
Beneath the Earth's vast surface
Till its head is thrust so high
It looks as if it's slowly
Being swallowed by the sky.
Nothing's too small to matter,
Too hopeless to be of need;
Even the wee prayers of a child—
God hears like a mighty roar.

Silent Rain

There is no thunder or flash,
Just a silent rain
That spills softly from the clouds
In silvery veins,
Just a cold, soggy drizzle
That dampens the heart,
Then slowly, and mercilessly
Rips it apart.
The sky hangs like a curtain
Lessening the light,
Turning our world as solemn
As the darkest night.
The wind is far too feeble,
Singing without sound,
To scatter fallen leaves, so
Pastes them to the ground
Where they lay in wet and cold—
Each must pay their due,
If they wish to fly away
Into a sky of blue.
The rain seems never-ending,
Soon it will be morn.
Will it pass, or is this just
The quiet before the storm?

The Ocean

A wave curls over the ocean
Then crashes on the rocks below—
The sprays of white clouds in the air,
Like a shattered fireworks display.
The force between Earth, Moon, and Sun
Triggers the rise and fall of tides,
And the winds cause ocean water
To move in waves, ripples, or swells.
The ocean claims most of our Globe,
Only the sky can boast much more.
Its beautiful deep blue waters
Hold ancient secrets and legends
Of mermaids, monsters, and sirens
That some say still live there today.
Below the waters, a garden
Of coral reef, seagrass, and kelp—
A tasty treat for sea creatures
That swim in their aquatic world.
There's also a water museum
Teemed with treasures from years ago,
That tell the maritime stories
Of the ships and sailors buried
When the ocean swallowed their souls.

Approaching Storm

A tangle of fiery veins lights the sky,
And the loud belch of rolling thunder
Heralds a pending storm.
The birds and squirrels take heed
As the air pressure drops.
They scour the ground for food,
Before seeking shelter
In dense shrubs or dreys.
Clouds as dark as soot
Race across the sky,
And the lake wrinkles
As the wind rushes overhead.
The air grows still and eerie,
And the sky turns sickly green.
A bolt of lightning sparks the sky,
Followed by a clap of thunder;
And the Earth trembles
As it waits for the storm to pass.

Hurakan

From the depths of the warm, blue sea
Hurakan ascends, riding the air above
And reigning as Heart of the Sky,
But soon he will come down from the clouds
On his one leg and foot flanked with claws
To wreak havoc on all he sees.
As the air heats and rises,
The pressure begins to drop.
The air cools and condenses,
And the rain falls from the clouds.
Small storms begin to gather,
Careless and uncertain
As they struggle to stay alive.
The winds begin to strengthen
And the clouds become one storm.
As the Earth spins, causing the air to spiral,
Hurakan directs the winds with his arms,
Waving them madly counterclockwise
Faster and faster, forming an eye,
 And as it centers, he makes landfall.
The wind pushes the water ashore
Destroying the land and all in its path,
Until Hurakan tires and returns back to sea.

Force of Nature

There is nothing more majestic
than the sky, the land, the sea;
Each the holy wonder
God intended them to be.
Yet the sky can split wide-open
and swallow up the sun,
As its spit becomes a torrent
that threatens everyone.
The land can suffer tremors
that tear apart the ground,
And make a building tumble,
wreaking turmoil all around.
And the sea can be a monster,
driving waves upon the shore,
fierce enough to sink a ship
as deep as the ocean floor.
In everything created,
a force of nature lies
that we must reckon with
until the day we die.
But if we live in shadow,
we will never see the Light
that constantly surrounds us,
even in our darkest night.

The Tree

The tree, once a timid seedling,
Is now prey for its timber
And a target for the flame;
Anchored to Earth by wide-spreading roots
That draws water and food from the soil.
Its trunk, a pedestal rising in air,
Cloaked in layers of scaly bark
To fend off cold, heat, and disease.
Its branches stretch like angel wings—
A home for birds and shade for all
Who wish to stay awhile and dream.
Each branch, dressed in finest fashion,
Dances with the gentle breeze,
And trembles in the storm.
But the tree that's firmly planted,
Can withstand the highest wind—
Each broken limb, a monument
For all that it's endured.
In the heart of every tree
There is a glimpse of forest
Which we must firmly plant in ours—
For every tree and every thicket
Bathes the air we breathe.

The Burning Tree

When the tree caught fire in the forest,
Flames gnawed at its insides
And smoke climbed its trunk
As though it was a chimney.
Its bark began to peel
And its needles shed like brittle tears,
As the fire scarfed up its canopy.
Its limbs crackled like a campfire
As they hit the ground,
Scorching the path where
Deer and rabbits once roamed and played.
Beneath the sun that now burns
A hole in the reddened sky,
Birds mourn their loss of home;
But where is there to go?
The fire spreads from tree to tree,
As though a funeral pyre,
But once the forest burns,
the seeds stored on its floor
Drink the rain and sun,
As its ashes feed the soil;
And just like Nature planned,
It renews itself again.

Fire

The Santa Ana winds rush
from east to west one early morn.
They sweep down the mountainside
And prey upon a low-burning fire in the forest.
Its flames leap high into the air and lick the sky
That now burns an eerie orange.
In no time at all, the fire is fueled by flora,
Sucked dry by the hot, high winds.
Smoke chokes the atmosphere as
An angry fire swallows the forest.
Pathways for escape are cut off
And panic spreads as quickly as the inferno
That erupts on the hilltop like a volcano.
The embers ride the downward winds
And spark more fires in the valleys below.
A town is reduced to ashes, and lives are lost—
Everything's destroyed beneath a blackened sky.
Whatever the cause for this unwanted hell,
Let us not point a finger—
But instead, mourn for what was lost,
Give thanks for what was saved,
And move forward to build a better tomorrow.

Nostalgia

Nostalgia   63
The Swing   64
The Porch   65
The Apple Tree   66
Remembering Auschwitz   67
Mother's Day   68
As Though I Forgot   69
A Different Christmas   70
Small Town Christmas   71
The Funeral   72
Somewhere in the Middle   73
After We're Gone   74

Nostalgia

When I hear the sound of laughter
Rolling off a childish tongue,
It always takes me back
To days when I was young.
When I look up at the moon,
My mind begins to roam
And I follow it to places
I used to call my home,
Where the scent of garden roses
Whispered in the air—
I cannot think of any place
I'd rather be but there.
When I look up at the stars
Shining bright against the sky,
I realize that one day
I'll have to say goodbye.
When I see the morning sky
Dressed in a gown of pink,
It makes me sad to know
Life's over in a wink.
While nothing lasts forever,
Who knows what lies in store—
But first, we must stop clinging
To a past, that is no more.

The Swing

The swing hung under the willow tree,
And oh, how I loved how it carried me.
As I leaned back with legs stretched out,
The sky came close as I swung about
The drooping limbs that swept the ground,
And oh, how I loved the gentle sound
Of the air that chased me in the swing.
I would close my eyes, and then I'd sing,
As if no one was hearing me.
And oh, how I loved to feel so free!
When I leaned forward, my legs would fold
Beneath the swing, and then I rolled
My back again to make it fly
Faster and faster, tickling the sky.
Though I held on tightly to the rope
As if indeed I dared not hope
That anything could ever be
As grand as swinging from a tree.

The Porch

They would sit there for hours,
As the light of summer faded.
All they talked about was
How much their bones ached;
That was their only complaint.
She would fan herself
And he would close his eyes
And slowly drift into a dream.
Whatever woes they had that day
Were forgotten; leaving room for
Tomorrow's toil and trouble.
Sometimes neighbors would stop by
And he would open his eyes
And say hello, as she hurried into the house
To fetch them a glass of iced tea.
The dog would raise his head
Each time he heard a noise,
And then go back to sleep.
The porch kept them connected
With each other and the world;
So, they sat there silently waiting
For their worries to be forgiven
As darkness swallowed their day.

The Apple Tree

It was years ago I longed
To have an apple tree,
But all the seeds I planted,
Just never came to be.
But my father always said
That one day, I'd receive
Everything I wanted,
As long as I believed.
So when the dog barked one morn
And chased away my dreams,
I hurried to the window
To catch the early beams
Of a bright sun in the sky
About to drink the dew.
As I looked out on the lawn,
An oak tree stole my view.
My father climbed the ladder
That rest against the tree,
And then he hung an apple
On a limb, just for me.
From his bag again, he pulled
More apples ruby red
To hang on every limb
Until just like he said,
If I waited long enough
My dreams would come to be,
And all I had to do was
Believe before I see.

Remembering Auschwitz

How could it have happened, I wonder,
Something so dark it shocks the soul;
Though done by those who were more like me than not.
I was not even born yet, is my excuse;
I cannot be responsible for a world gone mad,
A world that looked the other way
While the dreams of many lay lost in the piles of
Shoes, spectacles, and emptied suitcases;
Just as humanity lay forgotten
In the darkness of the World's consciousness
As smoke regurgitated from chimneys
And human ash scattered the sun.
But is it enough for only those who survived
Remember for us? We, too, must not forget;
So no one ever has to hear again,
"I wish there was something I could have done."

Mother's Day

The moon has come full circle,
Waxing now, on its path to fullness.
I feel my heart pulled in different directions,
Like a half-moon thrown in opposition.
Tears flood my face as I remember,
How you, too, stood between two worlds
Until the final moment
When you crossed into the Light
That darkened my earth and sky.
But now, when I see the moon
Split between the light and dark,
I rest in the peace of neap tide,
That keeps you ever near.

As Though I Forgot

I was there almost every day, and when I wasn't,
It was as though I forgot who she was.
And when the time came for her to go,
I felt like a burden had been lifted,
As though I forgot how much I would miss
Its heaviness in the days and months ahead.
Her birthday passed, then Mother's Day;
But soon after, my life changed so suddenly—
It was as though I forgot how to grieve.
She came to me in the middle of the night
When I was asleep, and I could feel her presence,
But there was always a veil between us
And by morning, it was as though I forgot she was there.
Summer dragged on forever as I focused
On all the things that were going on with me;
It was as though I forgot about her altogether.
But this evening, I realized I had not forgotten at all—
That my tears were just locked inside my heart,
As though I forgot how to cry.

A Different Christmas

That year, there was no tree
With twinkling lights;
Or blue, silver, and gold ornaments
Hanging from every branch.
There were no hidden presents
Waiting to be wrapped in paper
And bright-colored ribbons.
The walls did not swell
With the sound of beautiful carols,
No cookies were baked,
No gathering of friends and family.
As I walked down the halls
Of broken bodies and blank minds
Where no greeting was returned;
I knew Christmas had been forgotten—
Years of cherished memories
All worn away by time.
But even on the bleakest Christmas,
When all the rituals are ignored—
The hope and peace of Christmas
Can still fill the heart
And toll as loudly as a bell;
If only we let it ring.

Small Town Christmas

How merry is a small-town Christmas,
When the land's all covered in snow,
And people come to your door to carol
To help rid the world of its woe.
And the stars peek through the ruffled clouds
As they listen to the chorus
And people gather around the tree,
Cut down from a nearby forest,
To share good tidings and peace on Earth
While they gaze at the twinkling lights
That line every roof in the town—
And oh, what a beautiful sight.
And the frost on the ground sparkles like
Diamonds winking at the moon,
And the evergreens line up to dance
In their stylish snow-skirt costumes.
Soon the old church bells begin to ring
And everyone stops to listen,
While snowflakes fall softly from Heaven,
Like stars in the sky that glisten.

The Funeral

It was so long ago—it seems like a blur.
But she was the only one I remembered,
And ever since, I've always wondered—why her?
Why her, out of all the people gathered there?
So many of them standing against the wall
Were neighbors and friends I had known all my life,
Yet, I'd never felt so lost, lonely, and small.
I saw the lady sitting by the coffin,
Tenderly holding the hand of my brother
Her grief had transformed her overnight, it seemed,
For I no longer recognized my mother.
How could a heart so bereaved have room for me?
And so I desperately sought comfort from
The eyes that avoided mine as I walked past,
Lost in the careless whispers uttered by some.
There were so many there that day; why do I
Recall only the cousin I rarely saw?
All these years, it's haunted me, not knowing why
My memory of her had remained so raw.
Why there, in my darkest moments, had I felt
Her sweet, tender mercy as she walked my way?
I now know why she was unforgettable—
She's the only one who spoke to me that day.

Somewhere in the Middle

I scout the caverns of my mind,
Extracting stories from long ago
Which I can see more clearly now
That time has wizened me.
I fit the pieces together
Till the puzzle is complete,
And then expel what does not serve
Or should remain with only me.
I throw in bits of things untrue
Dressed up in royal robes,
For facts are never told as well
as lies that tell the truth.

After We're Gone

Long after we're gone,
Our lives will continue in the stories told
By others who knew us,
And were touched in ways
We never thought or knew.
Others will say things we often said;
Words that were funny, tender, or mean.
Some things will live on after we're gone,
Though we don't get to choose what they'll be.
Perhaps we did things amazing to some,
Stuff we forgot about once they were done.
Our stories may live forever, long after we're gone;
Simply because we dared to breathe,
To love, to cry, and be who we were.

Distractions

Carousel   77
The Violinist   78
The Archer   79
Song of the Highway   80
Mississippi River Bridge   81
Sail Boats   82
Shadows   83
Windmills   84
Flying High   85
The Tree Top Hotel   86

Carousel

'Round and 'round it goes—
Driven by a merry tune so loud and lively,
 it conquers the air.
The children run, laughing and leaping,
As if a Piper was pulling them near.
Time grows long as they wait
While 'round and 'round it goes.
Once the platform pauses,
They dash to get on board to find the perfect pony
To carry them away—
Standers, Prancers, and Jumpers
With beautifully painted heads and manes
Romance the public and wait for them to mount.
A canopy with rounding board is edged with tiny lights
That sparkle like the stars.
Scenic panels and mirrors adorned with gilded frames,
And faces carved in wood almost seem to dance
As the platform starts to move.
The horses begin their gallop
And all are mesmerized—
By the playful, rousing sound
As 'round and 'round it goes
Like a wind-up music box.

The Violinist

I listen to the vibrant sound
The bow draws from the strings,
As it rises in the air like melodic wings.
Its tone, as rich and brilliant as a shining light,
Or haunting, deep, and wanting, as the darkest night.
What is it, then, that gives consent
For every note we hear?
The violin is the instrument,
But it's the maestro we hold dear.
It is not the brush, but the artist
Who paints what pleases or disturbs.
It is not the pen, but the poet
Who breathes life into words.
It is not the knife, but the surgeon
Who makes an injury whole.
It is not the violin, but the violinist
Who gives the song its soul.

The Archer

There are days when things slow down,
When words, once plentiful, do not come;
When I feel frustrated by things at hand
And cannot see past disappointment;
When I long for the way things used to be
And I curse the change that is.
But even worlds that are destroyed
By war or devastation
Can be rebuilt, made whole again,
Even better than before.
And lives that have been shattered
By ways that seem unjust,
Find strength from all their woes
If they choose to seek it.
But there are days when all seems dark
And I do not know the reason,
Still, I stand as steady as an archer,
Ready to make my mark—
But like a skillful archer knows,
The arrow will not fly
Though string is drawn and bow is bent
Till I release my grip.

Song of the Highway

The monotony of the highway
is eased by panoramic views
of purple Appalachians
rising in the air;
And from their peaks and valleys,
ballads from across the sea
sill echo from the folk
who live among them still.
We quickly pass a moving screen
of gold and orange-clad leaves,
full of Autumn glory
as they rust beneath the sun.
Low-height split rail fences
stretch across the land where
goats, and sheep, and cows
graze the rolling hills.
The sky is streaked with grey,
the color of the road which splits
apart the mountain breasts
and winds its way between
broad, pastoral postcards
of farms and weathered barns.
As we move into the Smokies,
low white clouds wrap around
their shoulders like feather boas
worn by ladies at a ball.

Mississippi River Bridge

The steel arches of the bridge
Emerge like a cathedral up ahead;
Its framework of trusses like
Stained glass panels
Depicting the river and sky.
With windows down,
I breathe in air
As sweet as incense
Burning its way to Heaven.
Sunlight passing between cantilevers
Flickers like altar candles
Lit before a prayer.
And the hymn of the highway
Sanctifies my spirit, and every
Sin my soul confesses
As I skim the shallow banks,
Finds its absolution
In the holy muddied waters
Below the river's bridge.

Sail Boats

I would lie in the hammock on summer days—
The sky's blue reflected on the lake.
A soft breeze would tumble over the hillside
And parachute into the valley.
The dog would jump up on my lap and muzzle
The open book spread across my chest.
Soon, my eye travels a panoramic scene
Of sailboats gliding in gentle daze
As the wind lifts and billows their canvases.
They moved as if they were graceful swans
And then disappeared as they rounded the bluff.
I closed my eyes and daydreamed awhile,
As the waves lapped against the dock house pilings
Like a thirsty dog slurping water.
Not long after, the sailboats came back around—
This time, turning in my direction.
When closer by, I squinted my eyes and watched
While crewmembers adjusted the sails
That now seems like folded wings of butterflies
Waiting patiently to catch the wind.

Shadows

When the sun hugs the horizon,
It casts shadows on the ground—
Silhouetting shapes and forms
When they block a source of light.
Like ghost twins mimicking our moves
They always stay beside us,
Looming large when the sun is near—
Then subsiding by midday.
The shadow tells what time it is
As it moves around a dial,
But if the sky is full of clouds
Time suddenly disappears.
If a groundhog sees his shadow—
Then six more weeks of winter;
So if by chance the sun is out,
His prediction is unwelcome.
But shadows cast upon a wall
Create the best theatre
And all you need are both your hands
And some imagination.
But when the night is black as pitch
What happens to our shadow?
Who can say it's no longer there,
For only the shadow knows.

Windmills

Tall and stark, planted in the ground
Where forests once grew unhindered.
Acres of land laid bare, forlorn—
As if cleared by a raging fire.
They stand, lone distances apart,
As their towers punch the heavens.
The sun's energy warms the Earth
Causing hot air to rise above,
And the cool breeze that takes its place
Now flows as it powers the wind.
The giant turbines begin to moan
Like an ocean wrestling a storm
And flashing lights send a signal
To warn aircraft of their hazard.
Their massive blades spin in the air
Like samurais wielding their swords.
And many birds fall to their death,
As giant knives cut through their space.
And when blades spin out of control
Titanic towers may topple,
Or sometimes they will catch on fire.
And in the dead of winter's woe,
They often throw huge clumps of ice.
And so, it makes one wonder why
We would ever want to farm them.

Flying High

The plane taxies down the runway then stops.
Once cleared, it gathers speed.
We are too slow, too heavy, to lift,
and the runway too short, I worry.
Then suddenly, its nose is tilted in the air,
the wheels are up, and we leave the ground
and all control behind.
The wheels crawl into the plane's belly
as we climb into the clouds,
tearing through a tunnel of fluffy, white billows
that blinds us from Earth and Sky.
The thrust of engines increases
and lifts us higher in the air
until we reach a level lane far above the world.
It feels as if we aren't moving at all—
but for some, even the slightest bump
or noise can cause alarm.
Below, a patchwork vista of lakes and mountains,
cities and countryside snakes past in lazy streams.
Little by little, we lower,
and the ground is magnified.
As engines slow and landing gear drops down,
the giant wide-body gently floats to Earth
as if it were a feather instead of many tons.
The wheels scrape the runway,
and the thrust is then reversed—
as engines screech to a halt,
heralding our journey's end.

The Tree Top Hotel

The trees breach the sky
Like a high-rise hotel
with rooms on every limb.
Up above a skylight
Offers quite a view
And illuminates the lodge.
And down below;
An atrium for guests
Desiring still and shade.
The dining room is open
Each hour of the day,
With a menu, sure to please
Birds and squirrels,
Bears and beetles,
Morning, noon, or night.
And not far off
A babbling brook
Performs a symphony
As the moon and stars
Light the ballroom floor.
But soon the guests retire,
And drift off into sleep
Upon a five-star leaf.

Meditations

Searching for Me   89
Night Song   90
Altered State   91
Dare to Dream   92
Only Then   93
Loved   94
Morning Melody   95
Self-Truth   96
Silence   97
Be Still   98
All That Matters   99
Listen to the Vines   100

Searching for Me

One day, many years from now,
You will search for me
The same way I once searched for you.
And you will wonder where I am,
And why I didn't say goodbye.
Perhaps you will feel
An emptiness in your heart,
The way I did so long ago.
But if you stop and listen,
You will hear my voice
In all the words I wrote.
And you will know that
Nothing can keep us apart,
Not even the sky or ocean.
And you will find me
The same way I found you—
For you were my inspiration,
And all the words you gave to me,
I now give back to you,
Keep them safe within your heart
Until we meet again.

Night Song

In the dark of night, I dream
Until woken by a song
As it rises o'er the hill.
Its melody surrounds me,
All at once, I am fulfilled,
Yet its longing burdens me—
The song moves ever closer,
And then whispers in my ear,
I am instantly reminded
Of the things that I hold dear.
I can feel its beating heart
As its chorus captures me,
Removing all concerns.
And I wonder where it's been
Or why it has returned.
In my dream, a flowing river
Soon carries me downstream,
Then back again to shore.
Did I ever really leave—
For the song is evermore.
I can only hear its voice,
As it comes and goes,
I cannot change its pace.
Oh, I long, how I long,
To hear the song's embrace.

Altered State

I woke in the night
Being chased by a dream
And it made me wonder why
Reality seems like a safe place to be—
Though that's where dreams surely die.
To live in the bliss of an altered state,
Where all my dreams come true,
Is better than waking up from sleep
To a world that is askew.
Yes, I think it's better to fantasize
In the glow of moonlight beams,
And not truly know what life really is—
But only what it seems.

Dare to Dream

There are things I dare to dream,
Though they may never be.
Yet, my heart is filled with hunger
For what I cannot see.
Must I accept the truth
That's right in front of me?
Or do I dare to dream
Without apology?
As long as we are wanting,
Our hearts are never free;
There's only one thing certain—
Hope has no guarantee.
But I will not let go,
Or turn away and flee;
For all my dreams are filled
With possibility.

Only Then

Let each footstep bring me closer
To the place I long to be—
One that showers me with moonlight
And sprinkles me with stars;
Where the waves that lap the ocean
Are the song that soothes my soul,
And the gentle winds that whisper
Are the only sigh I know;
Where dark surrenders to the sun
That wakes me every morn
And its Light becomes the only Love
My heart will ever need.
Let the rainbow be the Promise
When faced with sudden storms,
And the clear blue sky that follows
A reminder of the Truth—
For only then will I be free;
Only then will I be me.

Loved

It was easy to feel unloved,
It wasn't just dark days
Of loss, hurt, loneliness, and fear—
But months, years, and decades.
I tried to overcome
My pain by excusing others
Whose love I always sought,
But that only brought me more pain
And kept me from the truth
 As I tried to fill the vacuum
That occupied my heart.
Why did I think they could save me?
When I'm the one who loves,
Instead of the one who needs it.
What was it, I wonder,
That made me put my faith in them.
But now I know the truth:
It is easy to feel I'm loved
When I'm the one who loves,
Instead of the one who needs it.
Love, after all, is always there,
All we need do is to accept it.

Morning Melody

In the quiet of the morning, I listen
To a haunting melody
Heard only in the soul
Of the one who gave it life.
I rejoiced that I still heard,
Though not as well as most;
And that the golden sunrise
Seemed more beautiful than before;
And that the words I write
Ring louder in my heart,
As if to let me know
That all will work somehow.
Perhaps it was my need for quiet,
God gave me even more.

Self-Truth

I cannot make a sparrow sing
Or change the sky to blue,
I cannot shift the winds that blow,
There's much I cannot do.
And when the rain becomes a storm
And I am overwhelmed,
I look out on the darkened sky
To see beyond its realm.
And when its rainbow does appear
I place my hope on it
And all the things I couldn't do
No longer need be met.
For all of those I call my friend,
Though we may disagree,
I wonder just how many friends
Can say the same for me.
Of all the things I cannot do,
The one I hold most true –
I will not change what's in my heart
To be a friend with you.
My world grows ever smaller now
And yet, I see its Light,
For only when we trust ourselves
Will our whole world be right.

Silence

Silence always has its say,
Whether we meant it to or not.
It can be rude or indifferent,
Unforgiving or even civil;
And sometimes none of these at all.
But it usually means avoidance
Of what we truly think or feel—
Unlike the peace that comes with quiet,
And has no other intention;
Silence has an echo that's
Remembered by the heart.

Be Still

Now is forever, yet we await
For every hour to dissipate.
We do not know what is in store,
Or if we'll like it less, or more.
The only thing that we can do
Is live each day in gratitude.
We must not fear tomorrow's sun,
No matter what, life will go on,
It always has and always will—
What can we do except be still?

All That Matters

I would leave today if only I could
And go where my heart longs to go,
High on a hill overlooking the world,
As I basked in evening's glow.
I would wake every morn
To the song and chatter
Of early birds all around,
And my heart would obey
Its call to prayer—
With silence, the only sound.
I would loll on my back
And gaze at the sky
As night pulls down its shade,
And nothing else at all would matter,
But the moon and star parade.
And all the dreams I ever dreamed
Of things that may never be—
As long as they fill my heart with wonder,
That's all that matters to me.

Listen to the Vines

Listen to the vines,
Perhaps they'll confess
How they came to be
Such a tangled mess.
Or why it always seems
There's more of them than less.
Listen to the vines
When you're feeling stressed;
Do they truly help,
Is anybody's guess.
All they will tell you is
Not to weep or whine,
It's not up to them
To tell you you're divine.
Just listen to them sing,
Till everything is fine.

Uncertainty

Kaleidoscope   103
Pandemic   104
Cocoon   105
Unspoken   106
Paschal Moon   107
Ironic Fear   108
Fahrenheit 451   109
Caged Bird   110
Dystopia   111
Sweet Liberty   112
Life, Liberty, and Happiness   113

Kaleidoscope

We never know what dawn will bring,
There's nothing we can borrow—
For, every day is different,
Either filled with joy or sorrow.
Life is but a kaleidoscope
Of everchanging views,
Like bits of colored glass
Reflecting every hue.
When we look into life's peephole,
The only thing we see
Are all the pretty patterns
We wish our life could be.
Yet it only takes a second
For everything to change,
And our life becomes uncertain
While its pattern's rearranged.

Pandemic

The sun never hides from a storm,
But the cloud can steal it away
And keep it from its duty
Lighting stars and moon at bay.
And the wave that curls in the ocean
Can tickle the shore with its play,
Or drown it without warning—
Casting doubt on us every day.
But behind every cloud, there's a blessing,
No matter what some may say;
For the Earth, even though mistreated,
Is recovering amid the fray.
Both faith and science are needed,
When we feel overwhelmed and dismayed,
For there's nothing more pandemic
Than a world that forgets how to pray.

Cocoon

Safe within my shell, I touch no one
And no one touches me.
Wrapped up in a spool of silk,
I'm safe, but I'm not free.
Before I isolate,
I do nothing else but feed,
Hoarding every leaf in sight,
To satisfy my need.
But once I'm all alone
And hidden in the dark
I think that I am safe,
But I am just a mark,
One who blindly thought
That all I heard was true—
How quickly I believed
The sky was green, not blue.
Many saw my struggle
And offered me a hand,
They took away the very thing
That makes my wings expand.
Now, stuck in my cocoon,
I'm anything but free,
I'm certainly not the butterfly,
That I was meant to be.

Unspoken

So much of life lost
In a world gone mad,
Fear and deception
Running rampant all around.
There's no place to go
And no place to hide.
No one bothers to question,
No one takes a stand,
And we fall, according to plan.
And the ones who never
Said a word, awaken
To a world unwanted,
But it is too late
And they find themselves
Staring at the wind
And wondering why
Nothing matters anymore,
Just do what you're told.

Paschal Moon

The World teeters on the edge of darkness,
Overcome with fear.
The human touch, now a lethal sword;
The streets emptied, grocery shelves all cleared.
Stores shut down, and people stay at home;
Lives Are lost, and fortunes, too, are gone.
Yet, the moon in all its fullness,
Passes over in the night,
To bring us out of darkness;
Returning us to Light.
Thus, the Paschal Moon reminds us
Of the Empty Tomb,
And the hope its promise carries
In every springtime bloom.

Ironic Fear

I used to wake and fearful
Of what the day would bring,
I'd look about in madness
And contemplate all things.
I was afraid of the light,
Afraid of the dark,
Afraid to be all alone.
Such a mad, and sad, and dark world—
That's all I'd ever known.
But now I choose to live my life
Unafraid and free,
And isn't it ironic—
Now, everyone's afraid of me.

Fahrenheit 451

Oh, all the fires they start
To force us to forget—
How calm the night could be,
Had we only listened
To all the stars above
Instead of all the lies
That we were told are true.
Now, all that ever was
Is nothing more than ash.
If we had doused the flames,
How better life would be.
But one day we will see
The Phoenix rise again.

Caged Bird

The sky is full of stars,
Some wander, some are fixed.
But none of them are moons,
They are just what they are.
We cannot dip our hand
Into a winding stream
And say that it's the ocean
Just because it's wet.
Nor can we think we're whole,
If when we go outside,
Everyone's a suspect,
Just because they breathe.
Our homes were once a haven,
But now we're locked away,
Like a bird inside a cage
With a hopeless pair of wings;
Unsure if we will live
Long enough to know
Just how much it costs
To give up being free.

Dystopia

The church bells no longer ring;
The choirs no longer sing.
The empty pews will soon decay,
With no one there to pray.
The children do not go to school—
"New Normal," now the rule;
All-day long, they stay inside
To isolate and hide.
The streets are just as lonely
As a darkened avenue,
Everywhere the doors are closed,
And rent is overdue.
The healing gesture of a smile
Hides behind a stylish mask
To make us unafraid—
But does not stop the enemy's
Power to pervade—
And once fear takes its hold,
That becomes its voice.
How quickly we forget
That freedom is a choice.

Sweet Liberty

My heart aches,
And I breathe despair,
As decay's stench
Pervades the air.
My eyes weep
At all I see—
The massacre
Of Liberty.
My tongue crippled
And robbed of words,
By those who fear
I will be heard,
By those who beat
The sounding drum
Till each of us
Is deaf and dumb.
My heart may ache,
My tears may fall,
But now and ever,
I stand tall.
And now and ever,
I stand for all.

Life, Liberty, and Happiness

Life, Liberty, and Happiness—
Three words that mean the most.
Nothing else would even matter
If these three things were lost.
We must stand up to the tyrants
That seek to take away
The ideas that we value,
No matter what they say.
We must never take for granted
Our flag will always fly,
Or that we will be protected
Until the day we die.
If freedom's lost, then so is joy—
We must strive to understand,
Our happiness is not the things
That we hold in our hands.
It is the truth that sets us free,
It has but one refrain:
We must always guard our freedom
Or it may not remain.
In ev'ry corner of the World
We are the Light that shines,
And that is why we must not fail—
For freedom is divine.

Disquietude

The Longing   117
Uninspired   118
Long Ago   119
Loneliness   120
Heart of the Refugee   121
Illusion   122
Dark Dream   123
The Open Wound   124
Caught Between Life and Death   125
No One Ever Knows   126
Travesty   127
Bitter End   128
In My Dreams   129
Awareness   130
Tears   131
The Wait   132
Differences   133
Uncertain Journey   134
Journey Within   136

The Longing

There is a sorrow I can't name,
I feel it all around.
Though like the cry of mourning doves,
It makes a lovely sound.
It matters not if I'm awake
Or safely in my dreams,
I feel its pinch within my heart;
As real as what it seems.
I've never known for what I long,
But like the air I breathe
I cannot live without it, or
Pretend it's make-believe.
It wakes me every morning,
I feel its tender sigh.
This longing deep inside of me
Will live until I die.

Uninspired

I had forgotten how to love,
And the moon and stars
No longer wooed me to the sky.
And when the sun rose
Its light stole away my dreams and
Left me drowning in
The darkness of my heart and soul.
Each day seemed like Monday and the
Seasons never changed.
The birds sang only solemn hymns
And the air was still.
Like a leaf carried down a stream
Past low-winding banks
Edged with rugged scrub and forest,
Life drifted along
But without any place to go.
I sometimes wonder
What would I be if not for you–
Just a rambling leaf,
Going nowhere, nowhere at all?

Long Ago

I never thought I could walk away
Without once looking back,
Or that my heart wouldn't break into
Each time I thought of you.
It took a lot out of me, no doubt;
More than I realized.
Time has a way of soothing our souls
By making us forget
But memories are only hidden,
Waiting to be dug up.
But now I can think of you and say
That we were never one,
But more like ships passing in the night.
I wanted someone to love,
But I know now it was never you.

Loneliness

There is a loneliness that never goes away,
That time and distance cannot silence,
Nor can any pleasure turn around
What seems so out of balance.
Oh, but I have painfully learned to still my heart,
And to never shed a tear,
To go about my daily life
By pretending I've no fear.
How sharp the claws of isolation tear apart
The wounds that have never healed,
Hidden beneath the skin of time
Invisible, yet still, real.
Year after year, our hearts are full of emptiness
And loneliness undeserved;
But not because we are alone,
But because we feel unloved.

Heart of the Refugee

Oh, Heart! Who thinks the World unstable—
Will doubt the Truth and trust the Fable;
Will hear the bird's song in the air,
Then follow to its nest, and where
The shadow of the olive tree
Feigns haven for the Refugee—
Who, weary, walks beneath the sun,
Desiring rest not easily won.
He sleeps—the shadow passes on.
He wakes beneath a perilous sun.
The shadow, never constant, has no Mind;
The Traveler, to its movement blind.
Oh, Heart! That longs to realize
The dreams you thought to be the Prize;
Your days, now numbered one by one,
Like shadows drowning in the sun.

Illusion

Is Life but an illusion created by our thoughts?
I sometimes recall what I can't remember,
As though I'm living in a parallel universe.
Yesterday was once tomorrow, but now it is today.
I wonder why I never knew that all there is, is now—
There is no moving forward or moving in reverse.

Does Death hang like a curtain dividing Dark and Light,
Showing itself in the wrinkled face and hand?
We die a little more each day until we feel its sting.
Yet Death does not exist in a timeless, spaceless World,
But like a tree that sheds its leaves in Autumn,
Each crumpled leaf portends its birth again in Spring.

Life and Death coexist much like the Sun and Moon
That share the same sky Day and Night, with each a role to play,
Dying unto Death, both specific and indefinite—
We live, we die; we die, we live inside a multiverse
Where everything's the same and everything is not,
Where Life and Death are evermore degrees of Dark and Light.

Dark Dream

I may have died in my sleep last night,
Or else I had a dream.
The world turned dark, and there was no sound,
At least that's how it seemed.
But then I heard a familiar voice
Calling my name out loud,
And so I followed, though I know not where,
As if I were in a cloud.
All I truly wanted to do
Was to find my way back home,
So I awoke fully alive,
Not knowing where I'd roamed.
But that doesn't bother me at all—
I made it through the night,
There's nothing more I have to fear
As long as there is Light.

The Open Wound

A small wound, if left untreated,
Sometimes weeps and causes pain,
And once it is infected,
It can fester and inflame.
And even if it's bandaged
A lesion can turn septic
And too stubborn to be cured.
Once blood becomes toxemic—
How then can we save ourselves
From impending death or doom?
Is there any medicine
That will keep us from the tomb?
It's not the pill we swallow,
But the prayer of our souls
That humbles us through healing
Till once again, we're whole.

Caught Between Life and Death

Some things were, but are no more—
The wave that washes on the shore
Then shrinks to where it was before.
The innocence of morning light,
That overcomes the dark of night.
The places where we used to go,
That pulls our hearts in tow.
Now is the only time we own,
Yet, we yearn for what's unknown.
And like the far side of the moon,
There, but hidden from our view,
We see all things as true.
The deepest longings of our hearts
Will forever there remain,
And all the harm we've ever done
Will always bear a stain.
Caught between life and death,
We long for what was or could have been,
And if we cannot have it now—then when?
There is nothing we have the power to save,
And nothing we can take to our grave.

No One Ever Knows

Oh, Life, sometimes you are too much,
I feel you press against my heart
Till it no longer beats.
I feel my breath sucked out of me
As if my lungs had burst
And I am gasping for more air,
But there's not any wind.
Can we ever really lose
What we never had?
Even if it seemed so true
In all the fantasies we dreamed of?
There is a sadness I cannot say—
It follows me around.
What if, why not, when will?
Some things will never be,
And maybe best forgotten.
And there's still a road ahead
Waiting to be traveled.
What if, why not, when will?
No one ever knows.

Travesty

Oh, for the days when I knew so little,
When the world was a nice place to be.
Now, bitter voices rise and batter my soul,
Where thoughts and feelings have long been stored;
Why did I not pay more attention
To things I saw and heard?
But now dark forces have escaped their hiding place,
Staring straight at me and mocking the things I believe.
What could I have done but didn't?
What can I do now but run?
Yet, there are so many of us trapped in this mire,
And others blind-sided who will soon awake,
Who will feel the weight the same as me,
Despite our opposing views.
Might we find our way out someday?
Perhaps that is why they don't want us to pray.

Bitter End

Sometimes she'd go to the window
On the thirty-ninth floor,
And she would feel the pavement
Pulling her down,
And even the birds
Coaxed her to fly with them.
It was all so enticing
To disregard Truth,
And listen to everyone else.
The car horns below trumpeted
Her fall to the ground.
And her body lay shattered
As if it were made of glass.
But moments before,
She tried to grasp
The ledge of the window,
But by then, she hung in
The middle of life and death.
And as she fell, she heard herself cry,
"Why, oh why, did this have to be?
Things were never that bad, after all."
But the birds were already singing
"Too late! Too late."

In My Dreams

I've stood at the graveside often,
My heart enflamed with grief,
And I've wept a fountain of tears
That brought me no relief.
The ones who have gone before me,
I long to see them again,
Oh, how empty my heart feels, as
I think of them in vain.
Each time that I look at the moon
Rising over the hill,
I long to see them in my dreams,
And hope they always will
Be there whenever I need them,
To steer me back to Light.
Even in my darkest moments,
I'll wait for them each night
To come back to me in my dreams
And never go away,
Oh, how I long for that to be—
If only they could stay.

Awareness

I once had everything I ever wanted
 and didn't know it
because I wanted more—
Was I disappointed too, in how the
moon and stars were all arranged?
Did I hear a bird's song
and think it out of tune?
I never saw perfection
in things the way they were.
I simply wanted more and more
no matter what was given—
but the only thing I ever lacked
 was what I didn't see.

Tears

The tears come at unexpected times.
My mind tells me to save them for later,
But my heart doesn't agree.
I tell myself that it's all right to grieve—
Even if it's too soon.
It just means I already know
How I'll feel when you're gone.
I will not let today become tomorrow
Without having said I love you
One last time.

The Wait

The night is made darker by the clouds
 that cover the moon and stars,
Lit only by lightning that streaks across the sky;
As thunder bellows the injustice of a storm.
I wait in awe of each fragile breath that keeps her here,
Though she is already gone from me;
And the prayers, long uttered, now change their direction—
With a new understanding of what healing truly is.
The words, I cannot speak aloud
Lie scattered like tears upon the page.
The sun that rises no longer brings me promise
As I wait, unsure of when the waiting ends.

Differences

I do not know your pain; only mine.
Or why I sometimes see a grey sky,
And you, a brilliant blue.
I do not know why you stay busy
During times of discord,
As though nothing really matters,
While I walk the floors, unable to sleep.
Or why you hide your pain,
Ignoring how tender it is to touch;
While I claw at my wounds,
Making them bleed even more.
Or why you never express your feelings
Even in your darkest moments;
As though that makes you stronger than me.
Or why you don't really need someone around
The way I do when I'm feeling down,
As if that makes me incomplete somehow.
Are we really so different?
Does not the day and night
Exist in a single sky—
Yet, so differently expressed as Light and Dark
As the Earth rotates on its axis.
I think that deep within our hearts,
When our dreams become disappointments—
No matter how different we are,
We all weep the same.

Uncertain Journey

Hanging upside down one moment,
Tethered only by a silk swathe below my waist,
A gentle breeze swooped my face
As I swung in the air back and forth;
Free of all worry and unaware of what would come.
A few hours later, my world turns upside down
And pushes me over its edge.
The walls pursue me, and the ceiling spins,
As my life hangs in the balance.

Days of uncertainty pass,
My equilibrium, gone awry.
Weeks of rehab and tests—
Searching for answers.
Curled into a circular coffin
While a large magnet and radio waves
Capture images inside my head,
I find peace as if I lay on a yoga mat
In the silence of Shavasana,
Despite the one-sided roar of a beast
That cradles me for now.

When I pray, I do not moan or curse
That which looks like loss,
I bless what is as if it were
As whole and perfect as before.
And yet I know, if I must live
In a world of half silence,
Nothing will go unheard.
It is only the waiting,
The uncertainty of my journey,
That feels like loss at all.

Journey Within

I'm going now, where no one else can go,
Where nothing else exists, except inside of me;
Where nothing can distress or take away my peace.
I'm going now, where only I can be,
Where the wind's whisper is the only thing I hear,
And the moon's light keeps away the dark.
This special place of mine is not on any map,
It's hidden in my heart like a grave unmarked.
I'm going now; I do not know how long,
For there's no time but now, forever never was.
I may be back; I do not know for sure
Where my journey takes me, no one ever does.
I'm going now; I've stayed here much too long—
I must be on my way; there's nothing here for me.
But where I go, the whole world's mine
And I'll be safe and free.

Patricia Taylor Wells published her first book in 2016: *Camp Tyler, A First of its Kind* for the benefit of Camp Tyler, the oldest outdoor education school in the country, which she attended as a child.

Since then, Ms. Wells has published the following books: *The Eyes of the Doe* 2017 (novel), *Mademoiselle Renoir à Paris* 2018 (memoir), *LodeStar: Reflections of Light and Dark* 2019 (poetry), and *The Sand Rose 2021* (novel).

Her awards include First Place for Family Life/Inspirational Fiction in the Best of Texas Book Awards in 2018 (*The Eyes of the Doe*) and First Place for Poetry in the Best of Texas Book Awards in 2020 (*LodeStar: Reflections of Light and Dark*). She has also received eight awards for short stories from 2019 to 2021.

Since 2016, Tyler Today Magazine has featured Ms. Wells six times in its "Authors Among Us" column, which she helped inspire to benefit local authors.

Ms. Wells, who holds a BA in English and French, facilitated writing critique groups for the Atlanta Writers Club and Knoxville Writers Group. She especially enjoys writing poetry and draws inspiration from the wide range of experiences she gathered from her travels and living in various places.

Please visit her website at www.patricia-taylor-wells.com